Winter Lines

Daniel Healy

Published by Cinnamon Press
Meirion House,
Glan yr afon,
Tanygrisiau,
Blaenau Ffestiniog,
Gwynedd
LL41 3SU
www.cinnamonpress.com

The right of Daniel Healy to be identified as author of this work
has been asserted by him in accordance with the Copyright,
Designs and Patent Act, 1988. © 2008 Daniel Healy
ISBN 978-1-905614-57-8
British Library Cataloguing in Publication Data. A CIP record for
this book can be obtained from the British Library.

Designed and typeset in Palatino by Cinnamon Press
Cover design by Mike Fortune-Wood from original artwork
'Winter Trees' by Annette Shaff, supplied by Dreamstime.com
The publisher acknowledges the financial support of the Welsh
Books Council.
Printed in Great Britain by Biddles Ltd, King's Lynn, Norfolk

Acknowledgments:

Some of the poems have appeared previously in *Acorn* (U.S.),
Borderlines, *Bottlerockets* (U.S.), *Carillon*, *Chimera*, *Coffee House*, *Envoi*,
Fire, *HQ*, *The Journal*, *Krax*, *Moodswing*, *Obsessed With Pipework*,
Orbis, *Other Poetry*, *Parameter*, *Poetry Cornwall*, *Poetry Scotland*, *The
Rialto*, *Seam*, *The Ugly Tree* and *Only Connect* (Cinnamon Press).
Many thanks to Jan Fortune-Wood, Kevin Bailey and Sam Smith.
Special thanks to Férdia Stone-Davis.

Biographical Note

Daniel Healy was born in 1972 in Wales. He's worked as a tote
operator, apple picker and Big Issue seller. He now works and
lives as a bookseller in Cambridge.

Contents

to Férdia

Winter Lines

October

Morning
at the beach

a dull
pigeon-feathered day

among the stifled
sounds of water

the hard
chipped flint of waves.

Coast Line

It had seemed
out of place

that fist-sized
swell of flint

among the rock pools
& the waves.

One side
a cloud of stone

the other
a cold threat.

Yesterday

Thinking
about our conversation,
drinking tea,
you said that life
was lived
out of context
& talked
about the rarity
of a clear thought.
I guess you were right.
This morning
I drink coffee
& notice
that the fruit tree
is dying
in the back garden.

Haiku

Already autumn
rain
shivers the leaves.

Coming Home

To find the evening
stillness broken

by the echoing
slap of a child

deliberately stepping

on every crack
in the pavement.

Sunday Morning

Shaving in
the white basin

red drops
of blood

& the sudden
reflection

of my father's
face.

&

I am strangely
content

standing
& seeing nothing

but the black iron
stairs

slick with rain
above my window.

In False Light

Two birds cross the morning
braiding the air

in a pale sky
the black, imagined lines.

In November

With the pavements
black throughout the day

it is only now
in the arc of a streetlight

that the rain is falling.

Landscape

The morning
defined by rain,

a window,
the street, the tree,

branches
reduced to shape,

a thread of water
on the glass.

A Sketch at Breakfast

In a café
of early mornings
& dark windows
surrounded by figures
heavy with fried bread
& the lack of sleep
all listening
to the fat waitress
of pale flesh
cheap lipstick
& spilt sugar
as she read
the menu
like a poem.

November

In the park
the pencil sketch

of trees
line the path

in the afternoon
flicker of rain

the chill of streetlights.

Image

from the eaves
an explosion
of birds

dark splinters
in a grey sky.

At Evening

at dusk
unsure of the light

the night
assumes its shadows

branches
cross the river

amongst the small
sounds of water

the cold rises
biting the air.

Placing the Rain

A supposed
momentary
distraction.

In particular,
a late evening
spent

in listening,
in separation,

to the sound of water
on glass.

Detail

While walking
into the hallway

of the grey
terraced house

I notice
the fruit bowl

so carefully arranged
for my visit.

Fault-Line

In the corner
of the dark room

in the forgotten
cracked mirror

bright fragments
of a broken cloud.

Agoraphobic

Shapes that come in the rain
are multiple & various

a conjuration badly defined

of turned faces in the park
the swell of a branch

& uncertain memory viewed
through the instability of water

it seems that peace of mind
is dependent
on the transparency of glass

rather
than the liquid nature of trees

& the once familiarity
of objects
            becoming real.

November Morning

Coldwater & daylight.

A pale sun, black streets
in weak
persistent rain,

through diffuse light
the gaze remains,

with only the sound
of traffic passing

to bring a circled
soft variation.

Answerphone

On the tape
the hiss
like a broken wave

endless & static

listening
to your machine-
tooled voice

take its soundings.

Impression

frost cold
breathing mist
parkland crow
with a broken neck

a vague unease
black, red & white.

At the Bedside

In the near dark
the prayer beads
grow silent,

what were once
smoke-smooth
with habit

are unmoving,
solid with grief.

Threads

In the afternoon light
before the storm

across the sky
a trail of black birds

like a crooked seam.

In the Crowd

Watching
as they lower the coffin

only a dark unfolding

as umbrellas
blossom in the rain.

At the Coast

After the storm
the definite
stillness
of an iron sea

undermined,
along the edge
the rusted
stain of earth.

Fragment

On the train
by the window

a child's hand
follows the horizon

each tree & hill
a rippled finger

reading the landscape
like Braille.

Flint

Watching rain
turning furrows black,

a narrowed reflection
beneath a dark sky,

sudden threads of grey;
the field, flecked with stone.

Cold, as you leave

The ache of morning
pressed against my fingers

held against the window
deepens to the bone.

Returning, Last Night

In the shadows
the house
didn't seem as empty

as I listened
to the sound
of water pipes
trace the building

it is only now
you can see the cracked
off-white walls

the floorboards,
the broken clarity
in the blaze
of an un-curtained window

a bare room
in daylight, the stretched
view of silence.

At the Window

Watching
the returning birds
carve their black,
smooth patterns

I call you to witness
& turn back to see
the suddenness
of an empty sky,

the lowered cloud
& the first faint
spots of rain
flattened on the glass.

In the Field

A cold morning
chopping wood

my fingers clumsy
around the axe

I chip away
the fragments

& wonder
exactly when

the skill
enters the hands

like memory
held in the palm

I scar the wood
& wait

for that single
polished swing.

The Frost

Winter
has etched the fields

strong, deep lines
score the landscape

making clear
the familiar, the forgotten

shapes of earth
a carved reflection

in the pale
empty colour of morning.

Winter Lines

Through the window
past the frost

thin branches
measure the sky.

Landscape

Driving out past the empty
ploughed fields

a broken fence post
frozen to the sky

the cold, sparse lines
giving shape

to a fleeting memory
of the marks

that my keys had left
on your bedside table.

I Know

that you woke
with the light

through that
bare window

walked through
to a cold kitchen

& made
a cup of coffee

it's after that
that I'm lost

left wondering
if the rain

I drove through
has reached you yet.

Before the Mountain

The early
morning ache

of hard ground,
the clarity

of black woods,
brief snow,

a taste
of winter

resin, bitter
on the tongue.

Cold Morning

Beyond the field
a clear day,
sparse cloud, light

shadows move
on the river,

a stippling of snow
threads the way
between furrows,

an after-image
ripples the sky.

Haiku

Winter field–
the rippled
shadow of a crow

Image of a Girl

In the park.
In the first fall of snow.
In the melt of what was.

In the desire
once again to feel

in naked innocence
the coldness of her skin.

Late December

Passing by
the abandoned car
in the snow

its black
burnt-out shell
is reformed

with each slow
drift falling

looking stronger
than the steel.

Leaving

Leaving
the tower block

a woman screams
in the courtyard

brings a line of faces

like brief spots of rain
to their windows.

Littoral

This morning the light
wakes reflection
from the lake;
an imprecise
faint curve of trees.
To cloud the image,
a ripple of wind
through liquid branches
and the sparse
fall of leaves, combine.

Late Afternoon

When dressing
you placed

your fingers
on my neck

as cold
as the morning

when you laid
beside me.

The City in Winter

half-caught,
an image reduced

to a glimpse of snow
through a bedroom window

like the white of an eye
dissolute & slightly yellow.

Sketch

Through the mist
the sight
of those faces
in the crowd

as sudden & as soft
as mushrooms.

Sunday

A quiet waking
to unexpected stillness

your white hand
on the counterpane
bare walls
& a half drawn curtain

snow is falling.

A Winter Landscape

at dusk
along the river

a light snow
sketching the air

behind weak cloud
the graze of sunset

traces the dark
uneven spine of trees.

Mountain View

The remains of snow

telephone wires
stapled to the earth

a barbed wind

catches the panicked
wing beats of plastic.

Intimation

The rain, a bitter wind,
rinses clean the night

quick ripples of water
on black-inked reflection

in the park, a cursive
shadow, beneath the trees.

Aftermath

Out walking
by the lake

clear water
after the storm

sunlight rains
through broken cloud

a cracked reed
voices the wind.

In January

After the snow
a brittle sky.

At the window
I watch you leave

& see the cold
tighten your skin

to breaking point.

Planting

Watching them
ploughing the field
after the rain

each separate
pool of water
holding the sky

a shiver of light
before the pale blade
turning the earth.

Sculpting

The exposed
bones of an island

near picked clean;
a carved imitation

amongst the shallow
waves of grass.

Thaw

Black ice
in white snow
uncovered in the rain

unable to stop
the gaze returning

to that jagged line
of footprints
tracing the way.

Shore-Line

There's a distance to the waves
the movement of pebbles

grown smooth. Across the beach
the fading of sound

a cracked shell, almost lost,

the moment reasserts itself
in the cold flinch of rain on skin.

Belated

The light
changed
this morning
from grey
to blue
without notice

the way
your eyes
changed
that day
by the lake

that I forgot
to mention.